Love Song for Cleveland

words ray mcniece   **images** tim lachina

Book Design: Timothy Lachina

©2015 Raymond McNiece and Timothy Lachina. All rights reserved. No part of this book may be reproduced or transmitted by any means without written permission from the publishers.

Printed in USA, iSSN 9780990543558

To love Cleveland is to love her in all her gray and gritty splendor.
Yes, Her, for she is akin to Cailleach, the ancient weather goddess of the Celts, often depicted as an old, veiled, long suffering woman. Picture her here as a gray mustached Babushka doddering down St. Clair Avenue through the slush at dusk.

Yes, to love her is to love her in winter, when the tide of the sky turns and one can smell the Artic Circle clipping down over Erie's chopping whitecaps, when the thousand shades of gray pall all over the Northcoast from the Flats to the Heights, from November until May, inspiring this haiku from my Slovenian babica:

> *Grandma says, never*
> *put your winter coat away*
> *in Cleveland*

It's easy to love Cleveland in the summer, when Lake breezes ruffle sycamores, cottonwoods and willows, cooling afternoon ballgames and barbeques in the Emerald Necklace. But we chose winter, after the holidays, when there is nothing to look forward to but cold pewter skies, as our pallette for this book. Winter, where stark black and white become Cleveland gray, will test all our sincerest affections.

> *January morning,*
> *rain turning to icicles*
> *on gray power lines*

We found beauty in the sodden, frozen landscapes, in the creaking, rusting structures of this once mighty industrial giant, in the blanched wood rot facades and cold steel and glass skyscrapers, in the drab brick walls and streets, and in the faded weeds:

> *Against gray slate sky*
> *sycamore boles ornament*
> *bare branches swaying.*

We've come to embrace this city, where the crooked Cuyahoga cleaves the land, in all her decrepit and gray and now rising again out of her junkyard grave glory. After all, she made each of us who we are. And though there is no sun, there's a burning river running through my rusty heart.

LOVE SONG FOR CLEVELAND

You work, you work, you work, Buddy,

"work," word of immigrant get ahead grind

i hear huffing through me, my grandfather's breath

from Grandfather's Breath

gulls scatter out
even above Cleveland
smog,

whiskey island dusk

Cleveland's gray shoulders /
sag in another winter cold dawn /

til sun ignites rust

Cleveland, not pretty,
not trendy, not rust belt chic
we still go to
work,
work

black steel bridge
pointing skywards/
into unpolluted sky/
where the jobs went

layers of freezing steel sky,

Cleveland winter

three straight weeks / of Cleveland gray skies, /

mother's milk for locals

Light, I saw, could blaze golden, carrying me
away from Cleveland where it can sleet or snow
or both for more than forty days easy, clouds
sliding low and steady off Lake Erie in layers as
continuous as the shale that hardend beneath
the inland sea that once covered these parts
and receded long before The Holy Roman
Empire raised its pinnacles. And long time
before palls of smoke sagged down from stacks
of plants in the Flats, where haggard faced
steelmen shuffled off night shifts through gates
of mills into dawn rain of iron filings.

from The Sustenance of Light

Ghosting out over evening waves of Lake Erie from Wildwood Jetty where my teacher brought me to fish, sheilding me against chill wind of fatherloss on those cold Spring days, standing on those same gray stone blocks where we caught perch when the sun was as young as us.

Ghosting Lakeshore Avenue, ancient gametrail, into the gates of Euclid Beach Park, that portal from whence I came — carney Ray giving free rides to Dolores on the flying turns, and home on Navy leave, swinging her across the dance pavilion. I ghost dance the concrete footer where they kissed. I, too, became a wayfaring man — that wide water calling to go as far as the eye can see...then go some more.

Wanderlust carrying me to Carrickfergus, where the long road rolls down to the salty sea, and to the Glens of Antrim from whence those Celts found there way to Amerikay's Appalachian hills and hollers, then rolling up that long lost highway to these shores where they married Slovenians from the foot of the Alps — where I climbed the same Mt. Triglav that flaps on the flag over the Slovenian home on Waterloo.

Ghosting past our old house on East 151st, the umbrella shaped tree buzzing with bees, lawns dewed with Lake Effect drizzle, the hush of sycamore breeze, cottonwood fluff frothing the surf below Shore Acres Park where my sister swung me from a rusting swingset up to glimpse the horizon of this shimmering world and back. Ghosting under carved forest lintel of St. Jerome's, dabbing my creased forehead with holy water and inhaling old world old god frankincense.

Ghosting Waterloo in the twilight now past the "KA-BOOM!" mural, where Danny Green's Celtic Club stood before the mob blew it up during our Bomb City days, the Man Himself defiant amid the rubble — A vacant lot but for the green plastic shrouded camper parked in back, tomb of the Irish mobster. Mom once dated him, and Dad borrowd money, he never had to pay back...

from The Ghosts of North Collinwood

Around the bend towards the swinging bridge
a fourteen story concrete grain silo stands, still in use,
two Foodland semis idle in the gravel lot alongside,
and next to it an old wooden mill panelled with 2x4x8 slats
painted with faded block letters REMEMBER —
the logo and product below it unintelligible ghosts
so there is only REMEMBER hanging there in the dusk
as I make my way back to Hoople's bar through stands
of weeds — thistles' tattered brown crowns,
bleached empty mouths of milkweed pods, sere hair fescue,
clumps of russet rushes, brittle ironweed stalks
and strands of rebar arcing up from fill dirt.

Something startles the gulls into a whirlwind again,
their squalling recalling the river before stacks billowed
and church spires staked their claims on the workers' souls
in their company houses lining the cliff rim above,
before toxic leak of this fallen industrial giant's
corroded arteries, before even the river muttering "Cuyahoga"
from it's crooked mouth, recalling this birth canal that
bore us into the world, this thaw flow that will heal over all
we ever were, all we ever will be, the ancient sea rising again.

from Cuyahoga Thaw

The city sinks like a gray and rusty
ore freighter moored at the shores
of Lake Erie. Sundown breaks through
like some ancient blast furnace.
What built this city but steel mills,
ore from Mesachbe Range
lakeboated in and melted down
with high-sulfer coal from Appalachia,
here where ancient Native game trails crossed.

from Always Leaving Cleveland

One drop of Lake Erie
wave crash over broken
concrete break wall
flares up and fills
with spring sunset
anointing my forehead
so I no longer see
hazy downtown skyline
along the western horizon,
but gaze through ozone
back to the beginnings
when the forest city
was still mostly forest.

from Cleveland Sunset

Late December grinds on down.
The sky stops, slate on slate,
scatters a cold light of snow
across a field of brittle weeds.

from Winter Solstice

The Bridge, Cleveland
FOR HART CRANE

Sitting at center span, breathing
panorama from Detroit-Superior Bridge,
between East and West
sides of Cleveland, between old border of United States
and Indian Territories,
watching autumn sun sinking over Lake Erie,
like a battered Brown's Helmet,
like the last tomato in an urban garden,
like the last ingot of molten steel fresh from rollers sizzling
down into cold, cobalt wave horizon,

last rays illuminating blue girdered underside of Shoreway Bridge,
highlighting Berea Sandstone blocks of old Superior Viaduct
like Roman Ruins festooned with gilded age rails running nowhere now,
and igniting this very nickel steel super-structure,
rivets like shadowy grizzle
of grandfather mill worker's haggard face,
girder I-Beam spine bending,
but still holding this city's once mighty dreams aloft.

I lean against rivets digging into my back —
that bit of steel in every Clevelander —
and revel in by-gone power of sprawling mills
turned dinosaur graveyard, blackened smokestack nostrils empty,
revel also in these dozen bridges still spanning the Cuyahoga,
once burning now flowing green again,
Cleveland's blast furnace heart,
still smoldering up river.
Cleveland's wall of red brick warehouses
glow along the East Bank, now condos,
glass and metal high-rise skyline shines in last light;

LOVE SONG FOR CLEVELAND

and the Terminal Tower — once second tallest in the world —
gazes to the four corners of the Forest City
under inauspicious skies bound to go gray
(winter in the back of every Clevelander's mind)
that curtain of rain into sleet into snow
making the lake, the city, the sky
one continuous pall
broken up by this sundown dazzle.

Seagull wings flash through dusk
as they wheel the flats
over mountains of gravel,
mountains of concrete rubble for Lake break-wall,
mountains of salt like ruined pyramids,
calling and circling higher
over the last bank skyscraper,
white crest glowing in the haze,
vaults empty.

In the 'hoods beyond, Cleveland closes foreclosed eyes,
grins busted picket fence teeth
on cracked corner streets,
as ghosts of post-war prosperity shoppers downtown
scuffle like weathered newspaper want ads stuck
on chain link fence around gutted department stores —
the poor bomb hit here first America,
we're finally #1! In poverty,
worse even than Motown's potholes
vacant lots and burnt out hulks.

But Cleveland still stands
even on rusting legs,
a tough town full of hard luck and broken dreams
where workers get up on cold gray mornings
and do it all over again;
not a Plum unless it's a bruise
from bumping into some bolted down machine
too big to be moved, no not a plum
unless its slivovitz to take the edge off another shift.

LOVE SONG FOR CLEVELAND

You're not on your knees Cleveland, never.
You're still standing astride the Cuyahoga,
from Carter Street Lift Bridge
that carries every train from the Mid-Atlantic westward;
from Shoreway Bridge overlayed on ancient Great Lakes game trail
stretching from Oswego to Duluth;
from Old Superior Viaduct, iron horse bridge,
foundation built upon Erie Indian trading camps;
from Baltimore and Ohio jack knife bridge
now and forever prophetically pointing skyward
through unsmogged skies
like the ossified finger of a millworker
showing where the jobs went.

And from this Veteran's Memorial Bridge,
when finished the largest steel and concrete bridge in the world,
legs sunk sixty feet in clay, arch rising
one hundred and ninety six feet above the river
and stretching nearly a mile —
once the busiest trafficked in America,
this nexus between East and West
over a river connecting North and South
going back to Adena people who traded as far as Mexico,
who built mounds where Euclid meets East 9th,
not far from where the only Indians left
play baseball at Progressive Field.

Just below where I stand,
near Lorenzo Carter's cabin,
the gate less Erie Canal lock yawns,
telling legends when rivers were roads,
when New York came to Cleveland by way of the Hudson, the Alleghany,
and Lake Erie to the Cuyahoga,
then turned South to join with the Scioto at Portsmouth
and from the Ohio to the Mississippi to New Orleans to the Gulf
where Hart Cranes' own swan song ended:
> *One arc synoptic of all tides below —*
> *Their labyrinthine mouths of history*
> *Pouring reply...*

I'm hearing his reply this evening, *complighted in one vibrant breath made cry,*
as he walked this bridge, broke again and back from New York,
sucking on a life saver candy
his daddy invented, when industrial revolution flames
scorched Cleveland's night,
when Minnesota ore married Appalachian coal
to forge steel that built the world
including this and his praised Brooklyn Bridge.
Could he smell the gasoline
Rockefeller poured directly into the Cuyahoga
before he finally figured
how to start the global petrofuel economy
from this valley?

Cleveland is crossroads of America
through Heart of it all Ohio —
freeway arteries now clogged at Dead Man's Curve —
Not even the winged Titans on the Hope Memorial Bridge,
the four Guardians of Traffic who cradle
a wagon, a train, a gas tanker truck, a luxury car,
can lift us out of this jam of progress now,
for further upriver the I-71/I-90 Freeway Bridge,
stanchions straining,
crumbles into the 21st Century
decline of the American dream Empire.
But Cleveland still stands as I stand tonight
on the backs of all those workers, hearing
Glenn Schwartz's electric blues kick in over
heavy metal swinging bridges singing below,
battleship gray RTA Bridge rattle-rasping silver cars over rusty tracks,
Columbus Avenue Lift Bridge, lowering slowly, sinking creaking
like Cleveland itself settling solidly,
singing its horn to Center Street Swing Bridge
that honks back to let a barge pass, *Cleveland Rocks*,
carrying a load of gravel, battered hull plowing the flow
like old hard-on of Industrial Age,
blowing its own horn
bound for St. Lawrence Seaway, for North Sea and beyond
to the mouths of the Seven Seas that carried
all the immigrant voices to Cleveland's shores
that join the breath that sings the strength and breadth of this Bridge,

chorusing Lake Effect breezes
swirling concrete catacomb ribs of old subway line below
and whistling cold blues of girders above;
chorusing echoes of paddles barking dugout canoes
through the place of the Jawbone
to muddy mouth of Crooked River;
chorusing blast furnaces roar and shift whistles 24-7,
with hissing smokestack sift and workingmen coughing,
knocking back taste of Cleveland shots
— one part road salt, one part cinder grit, one part fly ash, one part stale sweat —

chorusing that burning river combustion *whoosh!* signal flare
catching attention of the entire nation
and birthing green leaf flags of Earth Day fluttering;
chorusing also snoring veteran's from Nam and Desert Storm
who sleep in alcoves
under this Veteran's Memorial Bridge;

chorusing RTA bus rumble over ice-age potholes on Detroit,
slapping down ill-fitting man-hole covers
once forged right here;
chorusing piston missing beaters belching smoke,
and legs of hood kids peddling bikes towards downtown
rapping staccato bone-thug style;
chorusing kids bouncing bald basketball across the bridge,
tossing it into the evening sky, last glimpse of the sun,
chorusing grumble of laid off worker kicking crusted rusty c-clamp
that once held something in this city together,
across hieroglyphs of cracked sidewalk
and chorusing with the flutter of a single flake of rust
drifting down and slipping
into Cuyahoga's legato lullaby,
merging with the lives and loves and losses of Clevelanders
crossing from then into now across this very Bridge.

march sun on the sill,
translucent wafer of ice
floats in a saucer

city snow
dripping
from forsythia blossoms,
by boarded up house

equinox sky –
not one bird in damp, bare trees,
gray puddles still   still

flickering green tuft pushes
up through concrete cracks,
brings the city to its knees

I shovel snow
    from Cleveland
front lawn
    just to see
        green

a lottery ticket
found in the gutter grate,
the numbers worn off

from Selected Haiku

Love Song For Cleveland

Rusty guitar strings plucked by worn down, grimy ridged factory fingers
greasy with city chicken twang out this tune,
like a northbound train chugging
up from Alabama red clay sharecropper days
(and white sheet nights),
picking up speed lickety-split, kicking in
to rockabilly freeway go, man, go
from them hills and hollers of West By God, rockin' up routes 77 and 71,
before crashing beat on North Collinwood, Lakeshore Boulevard back porch,
my old man blowing summer harmonica breeze, spitting gritty soot from the flats --
this love song for Cleveland could easily be his blues

That same Labor Day off breeze
carries Slovenian accordion beer-barrel polkas
yodeled through Rechar's Hall,
Campo basso lullabies wheezing down Murray Hill,
Bohunk Old Brooklyn shadow of the steel mill waltzes,
and forlorn, concertina airs recalling Achill Island,
the fugue of all those tunes spreading out this evening
from western firelands eastwards to Appalachian foothills,
from the Flats to the Heights and all those blues between,
and settling over carp-back burnished sunset across Lake Erie —

the gloaming pierced by the eerie yowls of panthers
that once lurked through the Forest City
when it was still a forest, where wolf howls echoed
the ridges above elk-buffalo game trail that ran
just the other side of the East Shoreway's hurry,
and screeching coal train wheels on rusty tracks,
the same song lines the Erie tribe followed
to the Cuyahoga's swampy mouth,
can you hear their campfire hunting chants?

LOVE SONG FOR CLEVELAND

Can you hear Lorenzo Carter's Under the Hill Boys
swatting singsong malarial flies and wheedling brandy fueled fiddle tunes
that skirl into Navies' ditties as they dig the Erie Canal
at the foot of Superior Avenue, the tune merging
with shanty Irish rowdy dowdlings rowed back from Whiskey Island
up Collision Bend way, sodden gut string reveries for the oul' sod?
this love song for Cleveland could easily be their blues —

blasted by 1955 Lake Boat freighter horn
clearing the dirty air above swinging bridges
into swirling seagulls' calls
from slag heaps, rusty red pellets glowing,
Cleveland's pot o' gold hidden
under sulfurous clouds of Industrial Revolution —
at one point 15 tons of stuff per year was dropped here
on 9th Street docks where Gramps stevedored,
fresh off the boat from Slovenia after the First World War,
unloading the Mesachbe range iron ore forged into steel,
steel that built this city, this country, hell, the whole world,
from safety pins to I-beams to the very hull of that freighter.

Listen to din of Titan Mills whistling shifts,
silenced now, smelteries not even smoldering, rollers still,
dinosaur hulks groaning in the wind, collapsing
into piles of rust, or blow torch cut up and sold to China –
"Shanghai-ed!" curse the last union dockmen
into their boilermakers, creased hard working, drinking faces
laughing off lacquered Tremont bar surface reflecting
bowling ball trophies golden
as the suns nobody sees for months on end.
Soon their blast furnace guffaws will also fall silent –
this love song for Cleveland could easily be those blues…

ghosting along once empty Euclid Avenue Corridor
past bustling post-war prosperity chatter
through May Company, Halles and the Arcade,
before picking up squeal of St Paddy's day bagpipes on cold March wind,
catching that hip-hop beat at the intersection of East 55th street
and rapping all the way to Severence Hall's violins,
pulling as sorrowful as Warsaw ghetto kaddish,
then wending up Cedar Hill where a Polish Clarinetist from Parma
plays Duke Ellington's 'Single Petal from a Rose'
in an Irish émigré Jazz club

until it arpegiates down Mayfield Road to Little Italy
where old paisons strum mandolins
as beautifully mournful as the Virgin Mary
pinned with dollars parading the Feast of the Assumption,
before finally wafting out again from the shores of Euclid Beach Park
where my parents first met and kissed,
dancing in the pavilion to big band swing,
I listen now just as a cold front comes rolling in over the waves
as this chorus of muted steel cellos drones
the thousand shades of gray that pall over Cleveland
so gray it's the blues —

Gray of winter's dead snow, sooty piles that line streets from Kinsman to Ohio City,
gray of the aluminum shovel that sits by the front door year round,
bleached gray of beer can crushed
during some hot night, porch sittin', late inning Indians loss
and tossed into unshorn hedges as bare gray as tree line on opening day,
gray faces of tract houses from Euclid to Garfield to Lakewood
glowing by dawn's first light, set and determined to meet another day,
gray of cinderblock coal bins along Train Street in Tremont,
gray of 55-gallon drum of rainwater on the back of a gun-metal pickup
stuck with four flat elephant skin tires
beside a dull steel corrugated warehouse off concrete potholed Waterloo,
gray stink of shad kill along Edgewater Beach,
gray when driving down the Shoreway
so you can't tell the difference between the road, the lake and the sky,
if Picasso had a gray period Cleveland would be it,

gray of Harvey Pekar's hang dog face staring
into empty file cabinet before walking to dingy bus
rattling through Cleveland Heights' twilight,
gray of Daniel Thompson's Whitmanesque beard as he harangues
the specter of Rockefeller's empty tomb in Lakeview,
gray of the gray haired, mustached babushkas of Slavic Village,
gray of the frost on the lawns of Shaker Heights,
gray of Terminal Tower in the fog,
gray whirl of pigeons rising from Public Square
blending with evening,

gray summer thunderheads rolling in off the Lake
giving way to blue sky, high summer July day —
come March and the long gray march of winter
you'll be on your knees begging for that day —
gray skyline in winter that still calls me home to hymn
all these penumbras,
gray of the last plume from the last stack of the last plant
still burning in the flats,
rising like the ghosts of all those millworkers,
and though there is no sun this flame burns on,
there's a burning river running through my rusty heart,
this love song for Cleveland
could easily be those blues,
so gray, so gray, gotta be the blues.